Introduction
by Claire and Julie

Whether you've been painting for years or are at the beginning of your career, sometimes it's helpful just to step back and think about what is really important about face painting children and young people. Ideally you want to make their day, you want to fire up their imaginations and above all, you want to make them smile.

With the emphasis on fun, *Fast Fun Faces* will help you achieve all three of these aims. From experience we both know which designs children like the most, so we've come up with 29 exciting faces especially for this book. We also know that children do not like sitting still, so each design can be completed quickly.

As always, our easy-to-follow photographic stages are presented with clear written instructions to make this book easy to use. The designs have been chosen to give you a range of options which will please boys and girls of all ages. From snowflake fairies and colourful cats to scary skulls and plundering pirates, there is something for everyone.

The faces in this book have been painted by Claire and Julie using Kryolan Aquacolor, Interferenz and Metallic paints, in partnership with Charles H Fox Ltd of Covent Garden.

We hope you enjoy the book. Happy painting.

Claire and Julie

See our website for details and how to subscribe to Illusion Magazine, which is published three times a year: www.illusionmagazine.co.uk.

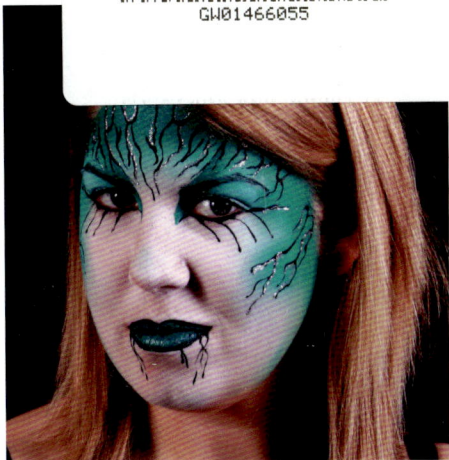

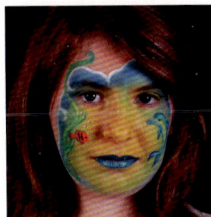

GW01466055

Illusion Fast Fun Faces!
Step-by-Step Guide to Face Painting

Written by Victoria Noyce
Edited by Claire Pick and Julie Oliver
Photography by Brian Oliver

Published by Illusion Publishing
15 Cote Park
Bristol
BS9 2AE

www.illusionmagazine.co.uk

ISBN 978-0-9555585-2-8
Copyright Illusion 2008

Contents

Contents

Funky Flowers

Model: Amy

Kryolan colours: Interferenz Perlmutt, Interferenz Gold, Interferenz RY, pink R30, yellow 509, green 095, white 070

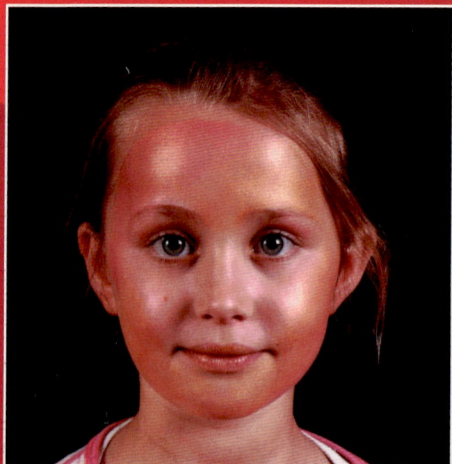

1 Apply a shimmery base all over the face, using light pink in the centre and blending into gold and rose pink at the edges. Add some of the rose pink over the eyelids to create an eye shadow effect.

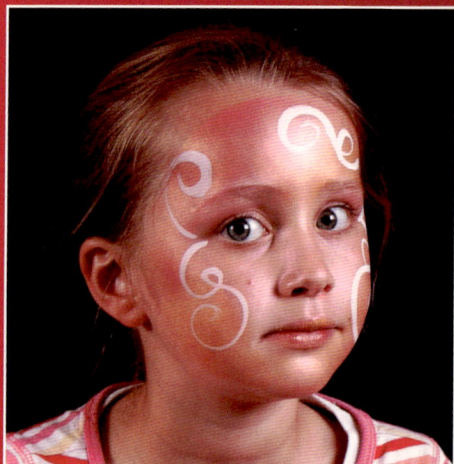

2 With a medium round brush loaded with white, paint a swirly pattern on each side of the face. It looks better if the swirls are different rather than a symmetrical pattern on each side of the face..

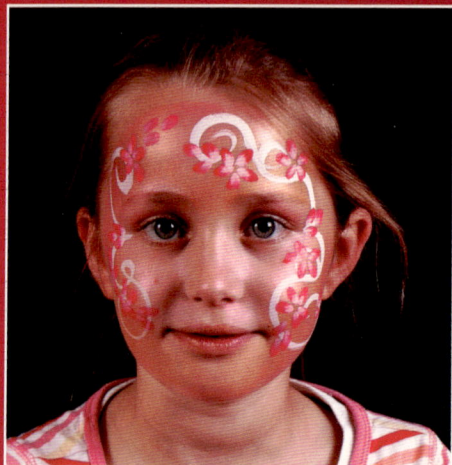

3 Load a filbert brush with bright pink and then dip the tip of the brush in white paint. Make flower shapes by pressing the brush on to the skin to create petals. Paint the flowers in a random pattern over the white swirls.

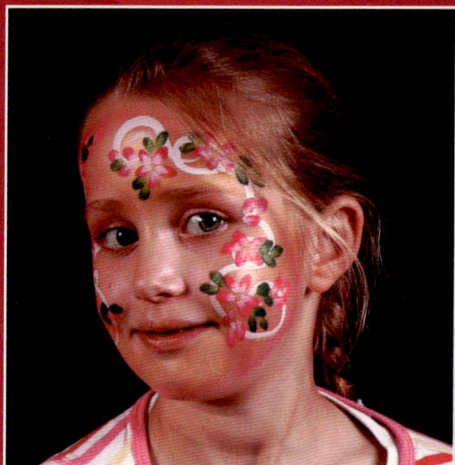

4 Load the filbert brush with dark green and dip the tip of the brush into yellow paint. Make the leaves in the same way as the petals, painting them in groups of two or three on the edge of the flowers.

5 With a fine brush loaded with green, add some more swirls around the edge of the flowers. Finish the flowers with a dot of liquid glitter in the centre of each one. Add white dots in small groups next to the flowers. Flower power!

Plundering Pirate

Model: Louis

Kryolan colours: blue 510, blue G82, red 080, black 071, white 070

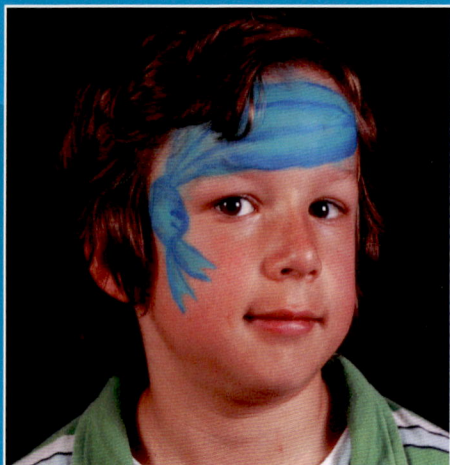

1 Using a sponge loaded with blue, sponge the shape of the pirate's scarf across the forehead. Add a circle for the 'knot' and two ties underneath. With a large round brush loaded with darker blue, paint the outline of the scarf. Add lines to the scarf to represent creases.

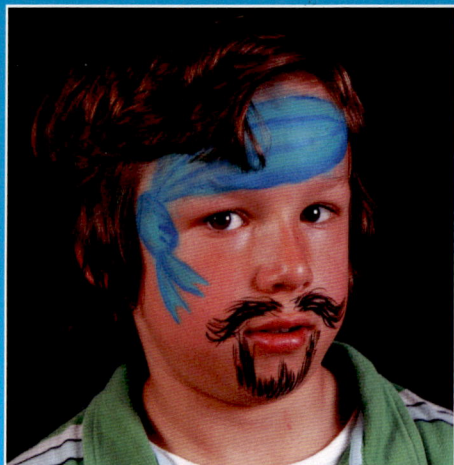

2 With a fine round brush, paint a wispy beard and moustache in black.

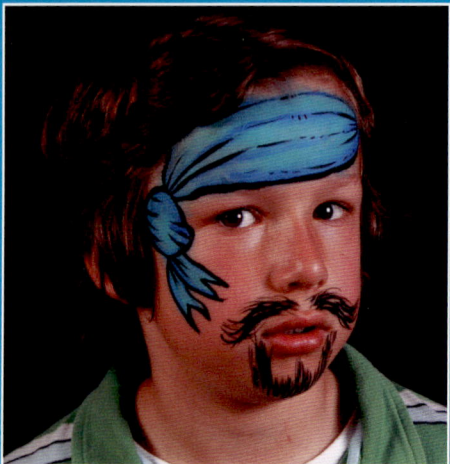

3 Outline the scarf in black with a round brush. Add dots and dashes to the scarf to emphasise the creases.

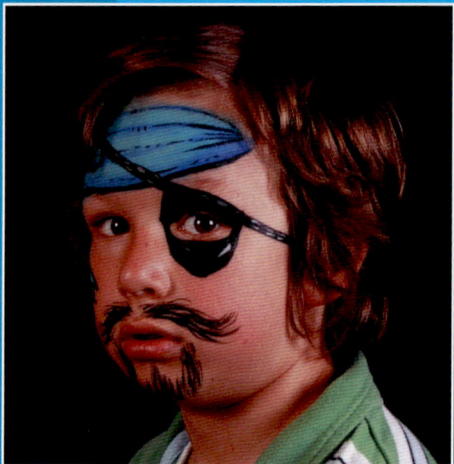

4 All pirates need an eye patch. Paint the patch carefully, not going too close to the eyes. Add the headband. To create 'stitching', paint dashes in silver and also highlight the patch.

Pretty Kitty

Model: Abigail

Kryolan colours: Interferenz Perlmutt, pink R30, red 080, green 095, black 071, white 070

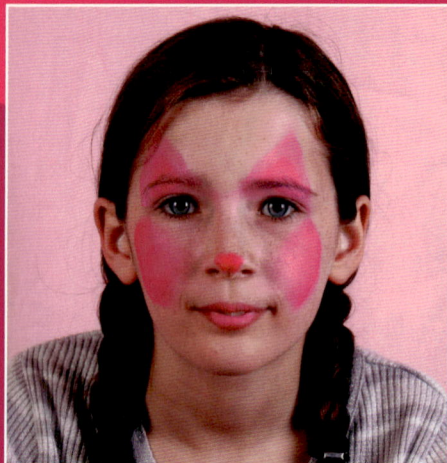

1 Sponge pink in the shape of a cat's face, including ear shapes above the eyebrows. Use a light pink shimmer on the centre blending in to a darker pink on the outer edges of the face. Apply a circle of bright pink to the tip of the nose.

2 With a fine brush loaded with black, outline the kitty ears and add three eyelashes to the outer corners of the eyes. Paint the edge of the nostrils in black and blend up the nose with a dry brush. Sponge white above the upper lip and outline this area in black to create a muzzle. Paint in a line of black from the nose to the upper lip and add black dots.

3 Paint in curly whiskers and irregular strokes on the edge of the face to create a fur effect. With a medium round brush, paint red circles between the kitty ears to create flowers. Add some black dots to the outer corners of the eyes.

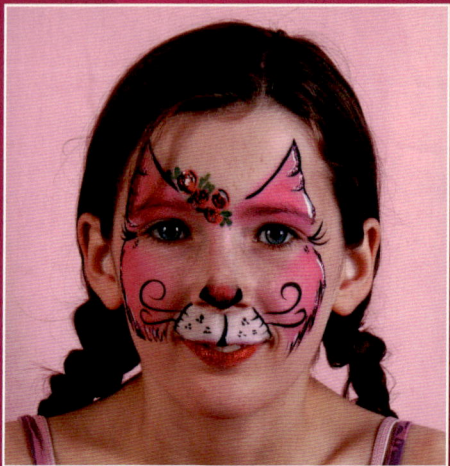

4 To finish the flowers, paint petals with a fine brush loaded with black and add small groups of green leaves with a small round brush. Add white highlights and glitter to the edges of the design.

Starry Witch

Model: Flora

Kryolan colours: Interferenz Silber,
purple R27, pink R30, burgundy Altrot

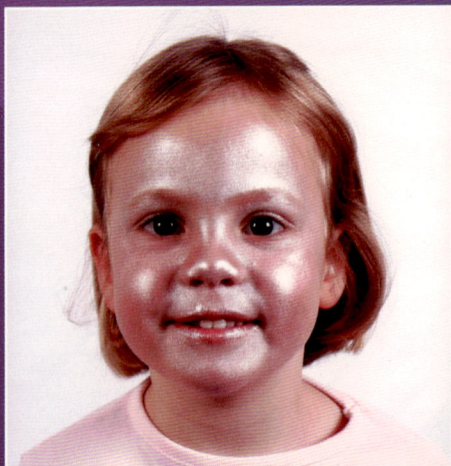

1 Sponge a sparkly iridescent paint all over the face.

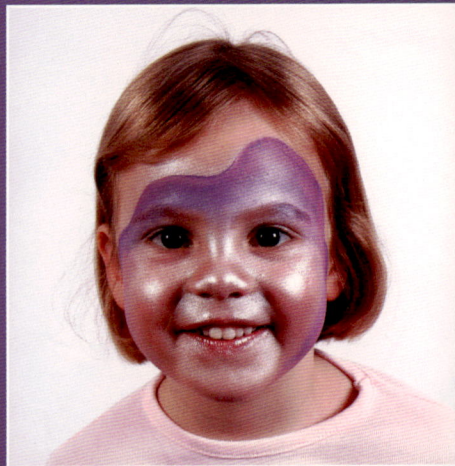

2 With a large round brush loaded with lilac, brush wavy lines on the forehead and around the cheeks. With the sponge used for the iridescent base, drag the lilac into the sparkly paint

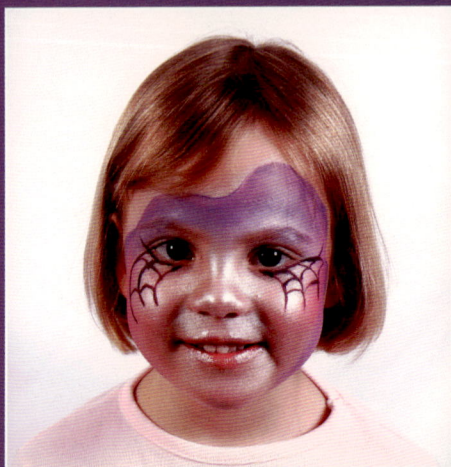

3 Ask the model to look up while a thin line is painted under each eye in purple. Paint three curved lines radiating out from under the eye down towards the cheeks. Join these together to make webs.

4 With a brush loaded with bright pink, paint stars next to the webs and also on the forehead. Add liquid silver glitter to the webs. Paint the lips bright pink.

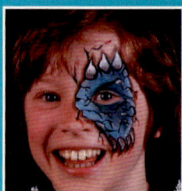

Dragon Eye

Model: Chris

Kryolan colours: blue G82, blue 510,
brown 503, red 080, black 071, white 070

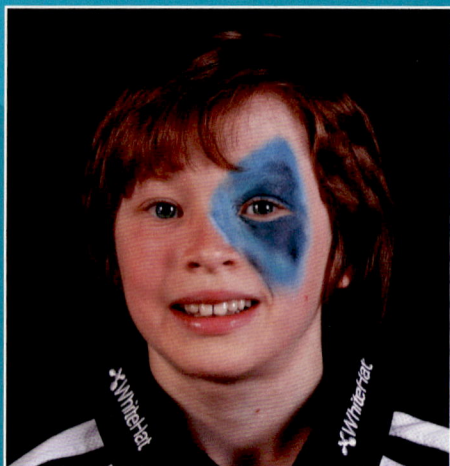

1 Load a sponge with light blue and make an irregular triangle shape over one eye and cheek. Stipple some black in a smaller area over the light blue.

2 With a medium round brush, create white horn shapes at the top of the design and teeth at the bottom.

3 Outline the horns and teeth with a fine brush loaded with black. Outline the blue triangle shape with jagged black lines radiating into the design.

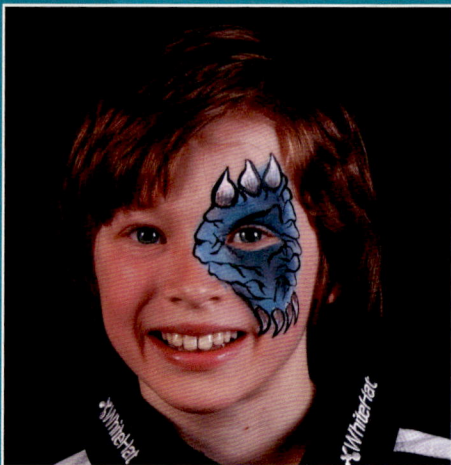

4 Still using black, continue the jagged lines from the outside of the shape into the centre of the cheek and add an arched eyebrow. Shade the base of the horns and teeth in brown.

Ocean Paradise
Model: Louise

Kryolan colours: yellow 509, green 511,
Interferenz BG, UV orange, white 070, black 071

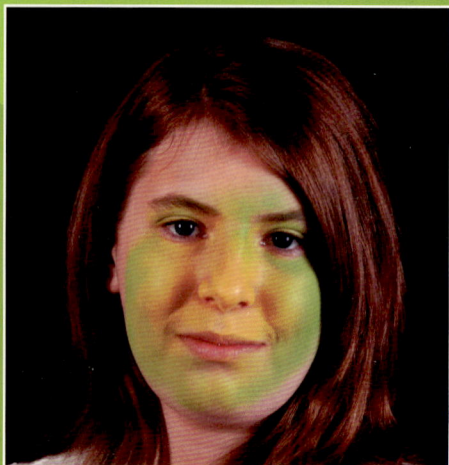

1 Sponge yellow in the centre of the face. Edge with green and blend together to achieve a smooth base.

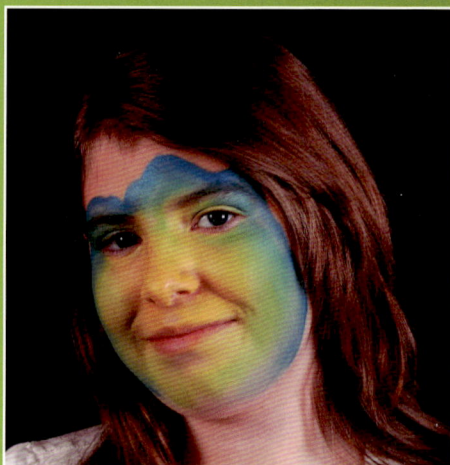

2 With a large round brush loaded with a shimmery dark blue, paint wavy lines around the edge of the face to represent ocean waves. With the sponge used for the green base, blend the blue into the green to create an airbrushed look.

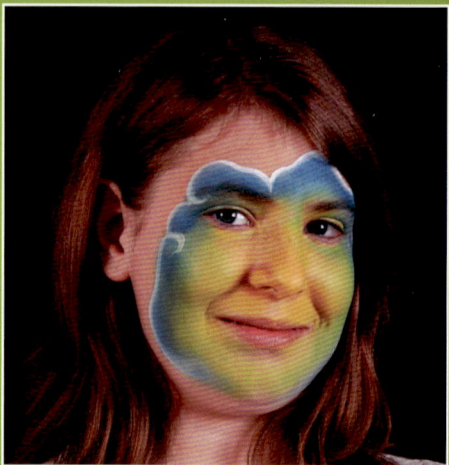

3 Outline the design in white and add swirls.

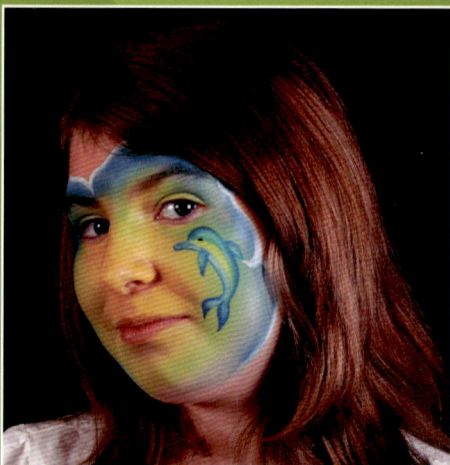

4 Double load a round brush with the blue and white and start to paint the dolphin. The first stroke is the shape of a comma going down the cheek. To create the nose shape and make the head and body fuller, add another smaller comma. Add two flicks for the tail and an elongated triangle for the dorsal fin and flipper. Add a small black dot for the eye.

5 With a large flat brush double loaded with green and yellow, paint swirls for seaweed. Add a fish of any design. Paint white air bubbles above the fish and the dolphin and outline in black. Paint the lips shimmery dark blue. Shush, can you hear the sea?

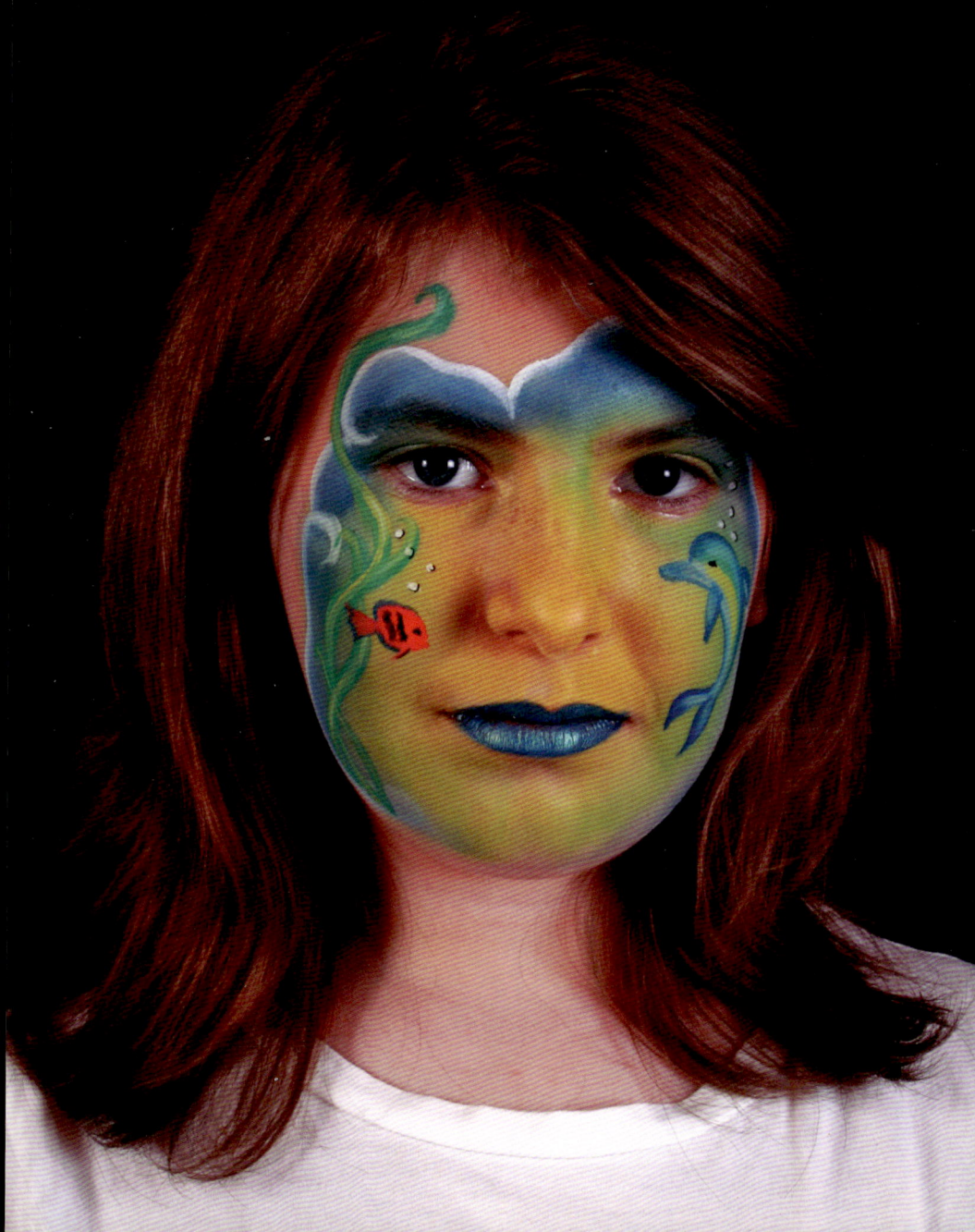

Me and My Mutt

Model: Fergus and Reggie

Kryolan colours: brown 075, brown 503, black 071, white 070

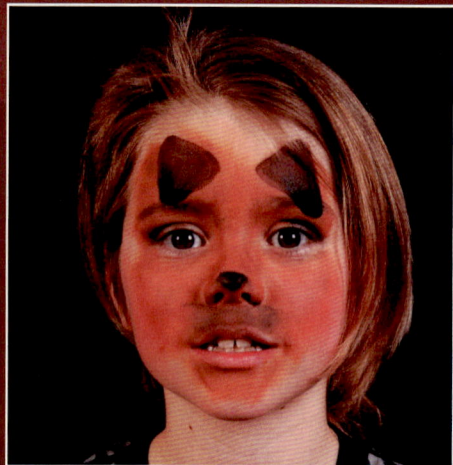

1 Load a sponge with light and dark brown, and apply a base in a rough shape around the face. Make sure the tip of the nose, above the top lip and the eyelids are darkest. With a flat brush, paint two dark brown triangle shapes on the forehead for the dog's ears. Shade the tips with black.

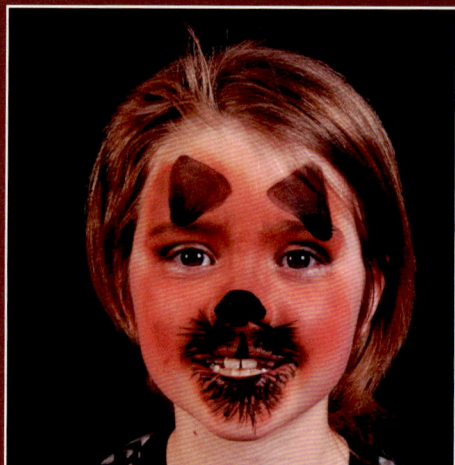

2 Paint in a black nose, and with a fine brush, add lines for dog fur around the chin and upper lip area. Paint a line from the top lip to the nose to make a muzzle.

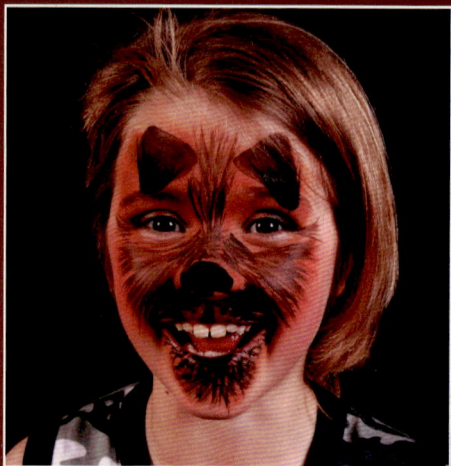

3 With a fine brush loaded with dark brown, add more lines over the cheeks and between the dog ears on the forehead. Build up layers by painting fine flicking strokes on top of each other.

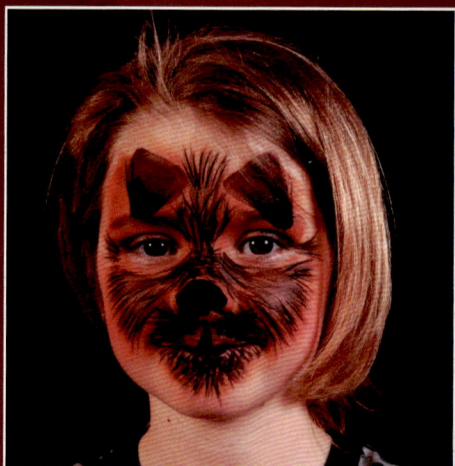

4 Add some fine black fur lines over the brown to add depth.

5 Paint in fine white highlights around the edge of the design, on the tips of the ears and whiskers. Add your favourite puppy to complete the picture!

Rainbow Queen

Model: Olivia

Kryolan colours: yellow 509, apricot R19,
pink R30, purple R27, white 070, black 071

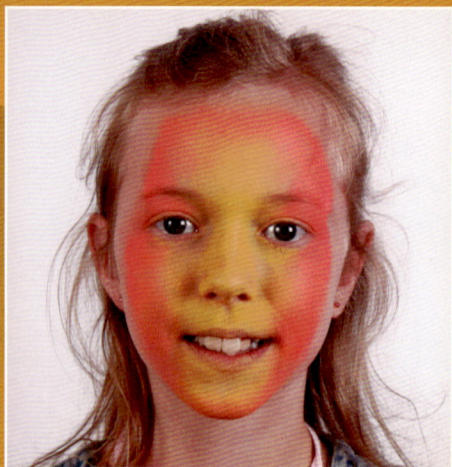

1 Sponge a bright yellow oval shape in the centre of the face. Apply apricot around the yellow and blend together.

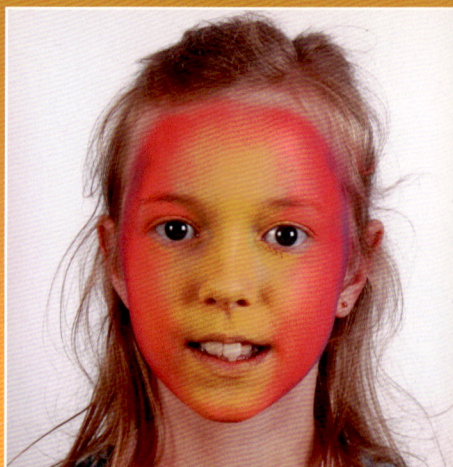

2 Sponge bright pink around the eyes, forehead and cheeks, blending into the apricot base.

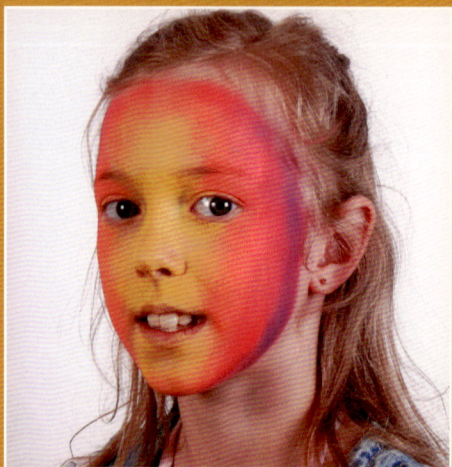

3 Edge the side of the face with bright purple and blend into the bright pink.

4 With a round brush loaded with white, paint curls and swirls on the forehead and cheeks radiating out from the forehead. Repeat on the other side in a symmetrical pattern.

Beautiful Butterfly
Model: Bethany

Kryolan colours: pink 03, pink R30, purple R27,
purple G108, green 095, black 071, white 070

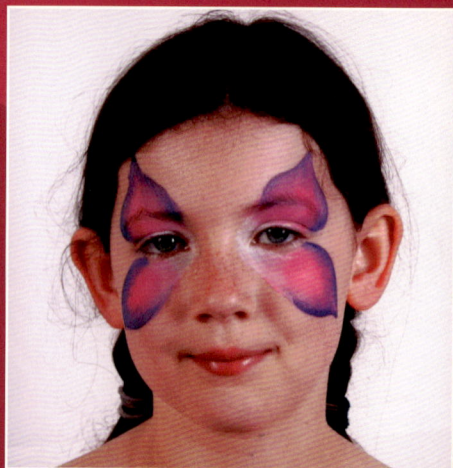

1 Load a sponge with pink and purple, and apply to the face in the shape of butterfly wings. Start with light pink near the inner corner of the eye, blending into bright pink and then purple.

2 Load a filbert brush with dark purple and then dip the tip of the brush into pink paint. Create flower shapes by pressing the brush on to the skin to make petals. Make a pattern of flowers across one side of the butterfly. Paint in the body of the butterfly with dark purple paint.

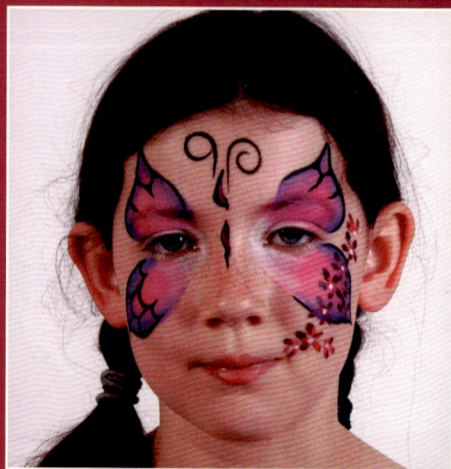

3 With a fine brush loaded with black, outline the butterfly wings and body. Paint in some curly antennae on the forehead.

4 Using a filbert brush, paint some green leaves next to the flowers and add some green curls and swirls. Paint some black and white dots on the butterfly wings and also on the body.

5 Paint the lips with pink and purple paint, then add some silver glitter around the edge of the butterfly wings. All ready to flutter away!

Green Goddess

Model: Maddie

Kryolan colours: green 511,
blue TK2, black 071

1 Apply green over the eyelids and forehead in irregular shapes with a sponge.

2 Load a sponge with turquoise and join the green shapes on the eye and forehead together on one side of the face. Add turquoise to the other side of the face. Blend with the lime green.

3 With a brush loaded with black, paint curls on each side of the face emanating from the corners of the eyes. The patterns do not have to match on both sides.

4 Make the curls more decorative with smaller curls, teardrops and dots.

Gothic Rose

Model: Jasmine

Kryolan colours: brown 6W, red 080, pink R30, black 071, white 070

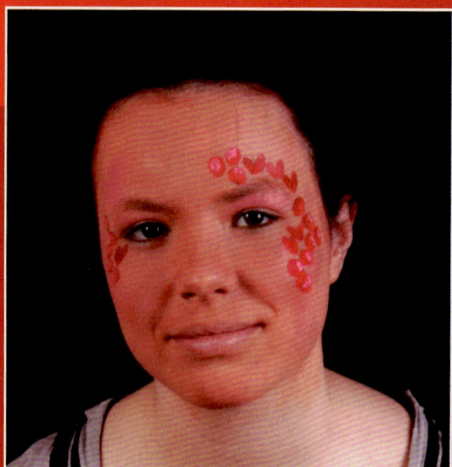

1 Apply skin-coloured paint all over the face with a sponge to create an even base. Using a medium round brush double loaded with red and pink, make a pattern of hearts and circles radiating from the outer corner of each eye. Make each side of the face different.

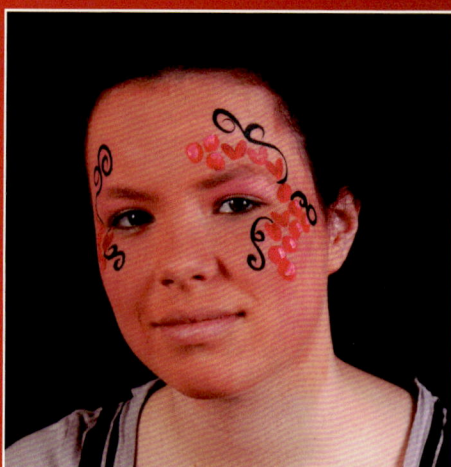

2 Using a fine brush loaded with black paint, add curls and swirls to the design.

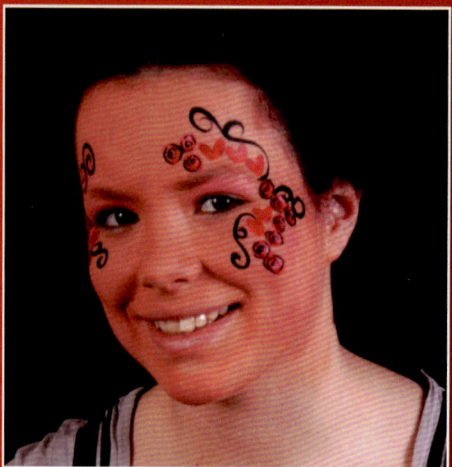

3 Outline the circles in black to make roses and add a swirl in the centre of each one to create the petals.

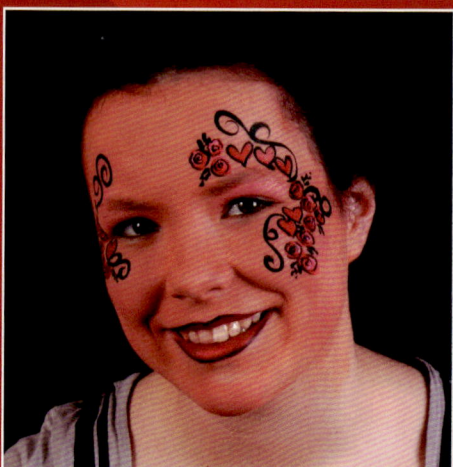

4 Paint clusters of small black leaves near the roses and outline the hearts in black. Paint the lips red, add a black outline and blend the black into the red with a dry brush.

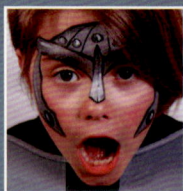

Noble Knight

Model: Fergus

Kryolan colours: Metallic Silber, black 071, white 070

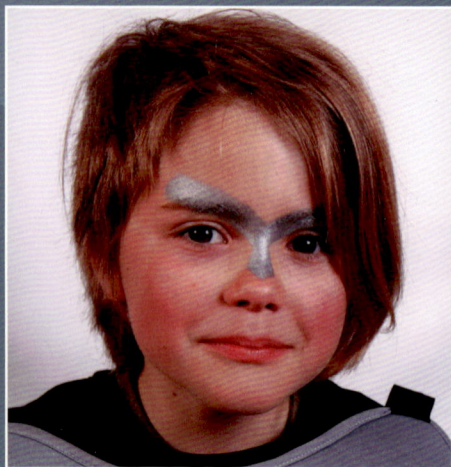

1 Using a brush loaded with silver, paint a large 'V' shape across the eyebrows and a man's necktie shape down the nose. The necktie shape should end in a sharp point.

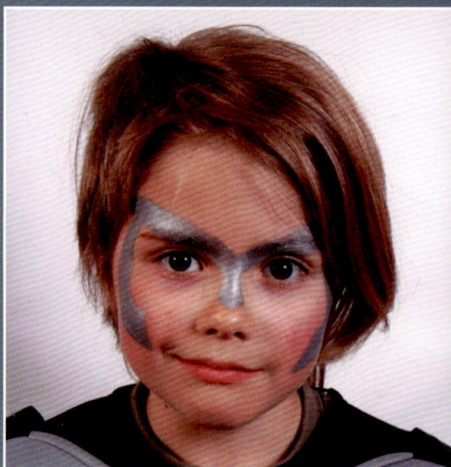

2 Following the contours of the cheeks, paint a thick silver line down each side of the face.

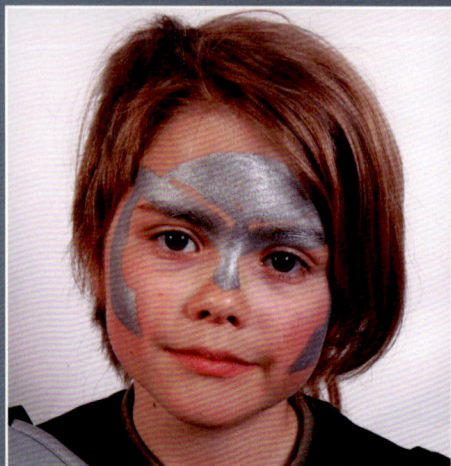

3 For the top of the knight's helmet, paint a crescent shape on the forehead. Connect this to the 'V' shape with a line at each end and in the centre.

4 Outline the whole design with a fine brush loaded with black. With a clean, dry brush, drag the black into the silver on the crescent shape.

Cheetah Eyes

Model: Holly

Kryolan colours: Interferenz Perlmutt, Interferenz Gold, Interferenz Bronze, black 071, white 070

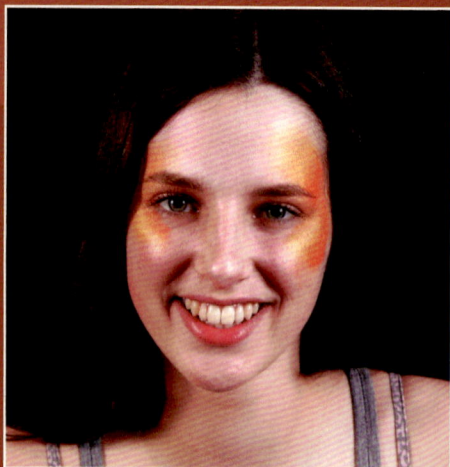

1 Apply a peach-toned shimmer base all over the face. With a sponge loaded with gold, sponge an irregular shape around the eyes. Add a shimmery bronze and blend together for a flawless base.

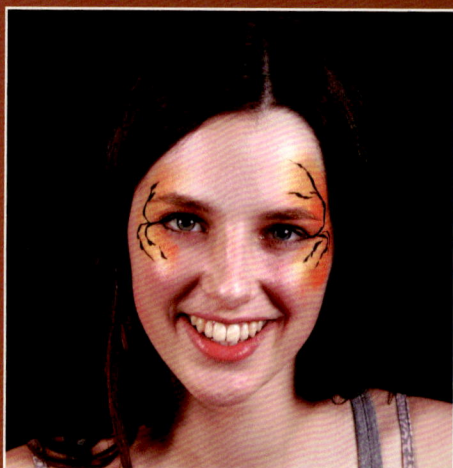

2 With a fine brush loaded with black, start to add details around the eyes, twisting the brush while painting.

3 Add open horseshoe shapes to create cheetah spots and highlight with white dots. With a brush loaded with bronze, add emphasis to some of the black lines.

4 Apply a shimmer bronze to the lips to give the design balance.

Crazy Camo
Model: Fergus

Kryolan colours: green 512, green GR42, brown 075, brown 503, red 080, black 071, white 070

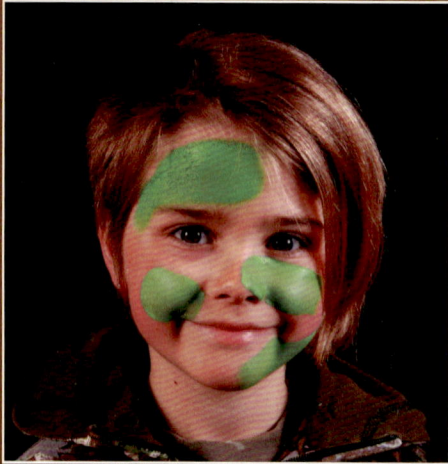

1 Using a wide flat brush, paint large, light green strokes in a random pattern over the face.

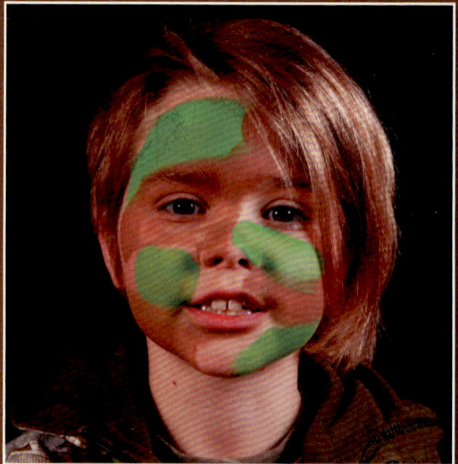

2 Load the same brush with brown paint and fill in the gaps between the green paint, leaving two or three areas blank.

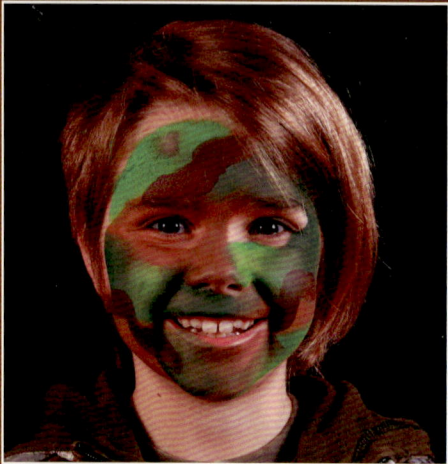

3 Add some thick squiggle shapes to the forehead and cheeks in dark brown. Shade dark green around the edge of the design and across one side of the forehead. Remember that this design does not need to be neat and perfect – the more random it is the better it looks.

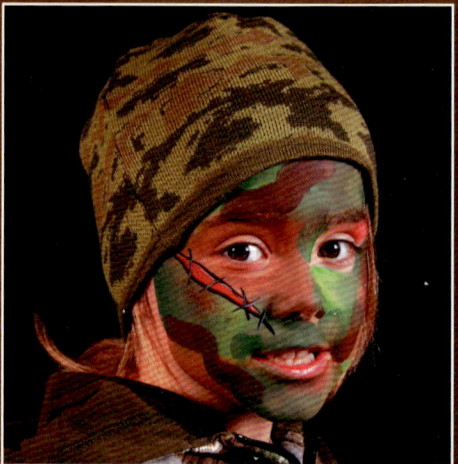

4 Paint a thin to thick to thin red line to represent a cut and outline it in black, adding small lines across the cut for stitches.

Patch the Dog

Model: Betty

Kryolan colours: purple R27, burgundy Altrot, blue G82, green GR42, pink R30, red 080, white 070, black 071

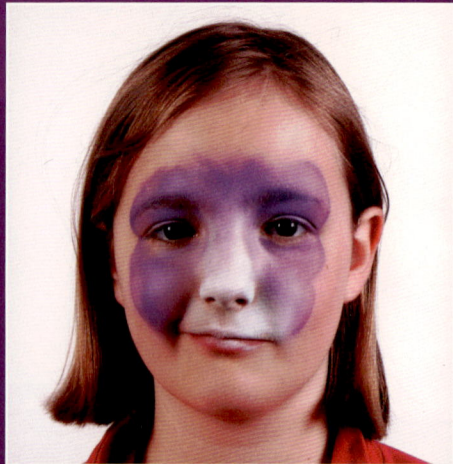

1 Apply a white base to the nose, cheeks and muzzle area. With a sponge loaded with lilac, create a scalloped edge on the side of the cheeks and forehead. This does not have to be neat as brushstrokes will cover the edges. Blend the lilac into the white.

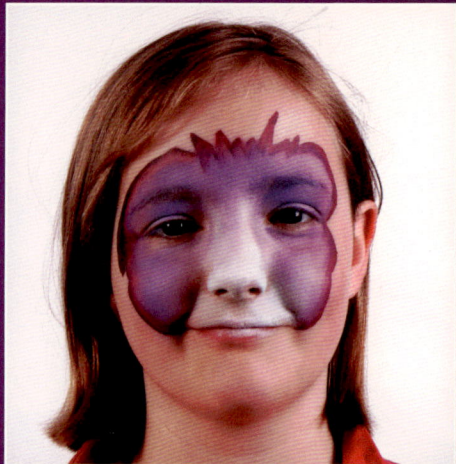

2 Load a large round brush with dark purple and outline the scalloped edge to the corners of the mouth. On the forehead, paint spikes to create the look of fur.

3 With the same purple on the brush, outline the muzzle and continue the line up past the inner corner of the eyes. Add a bright blue heart on the tip of the nose and outline in black using a fine round brush and highlight with white.

4 Add a bright red tongue on the bottom lip and highlight with white. Using a fine round brush loaded with black, outline the whole face, adding an extra line on each side of the forehead for ears. Paint a line between the top lip and nose for the muzzle.

5 Paint dots on the muzzle and add fine whiskers. Patch the dog would not be complete without a few patches painted on the cheeks and forehead in various colours. Highlight the design with glitter for that playful pup look!

Flower Garland

Model: Justine

Kryolan colours: Interferenz Perlmutt, Interferenz Gold, Interferenz RY, pink R30, pink 03, green 095, white 070

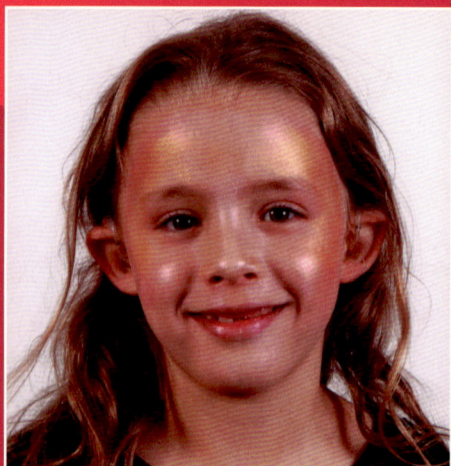

1 Sponge a sparkly iridescent paint all over the face and then sponge gold sparkle paint on the forehead, temples and cheekbones.

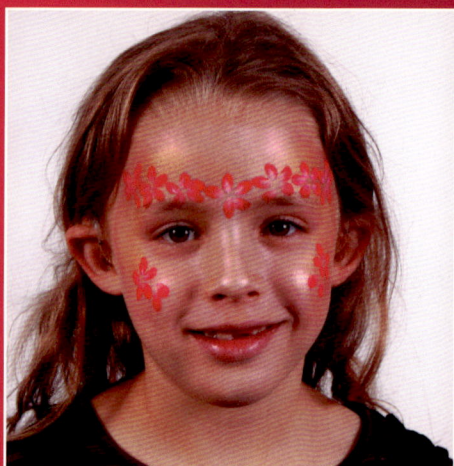

2 With a filbert brush double loaded with dark and light pink, make five petals in a circle to create flowers. Paint these in a line from one side of the forehead to the other and a couple on each cheek.

3 Double load the filbert brush with dark green dipped in white and make leaf shapes next to the flowers. With a fine brush loaded with white, add a dot in the centre of each flower. On each temple, paint a bow with trailing ribbons, making the ribbons thick and thin for a 3D effect.

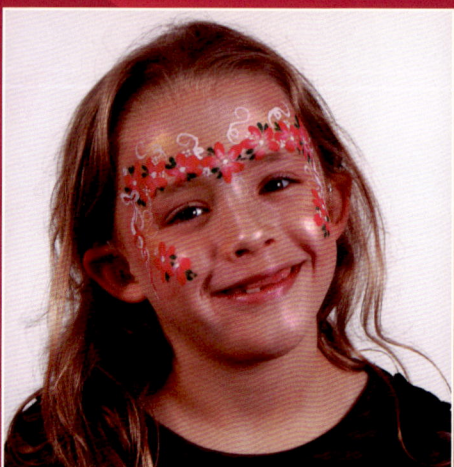

4 Still using the fine brush loaded with white, add curls and swirls and clusters of small white dots around the flowers. Paint dark pink highlights on the ribbons at the side of the face.

Totally Tiger

Model: George

Kryolan colours: blue G82, blue BL10,
blue 510, Metallic Silber, black 071, white 070

1 Load a sponge with three shades of blue and sponge a sweep of colour from one side of the forehead, between the eyes and down over the nose and opposite cheek. Add white to the upper lip to create a muzzle.

2 With a fine round brush loaded with black, paint in a small black nose, outline the white muzzle and add fine black dots.

3 Load a medium round brush with black and make thin to thick to thin lines to create tiger stripes. Paint the stripes radiating from a central point between the eyes.

4 Add white and silver highlights to the tiger stripes and paint small black dots at the ends. Add whiskers to the muzzle and paint the bottom lip silver.

Fantasy Flowers

Model: Ella-Rose

Kryolan colours: pink 03, pink R30, green 511, blue BL10, UV orange, white 070

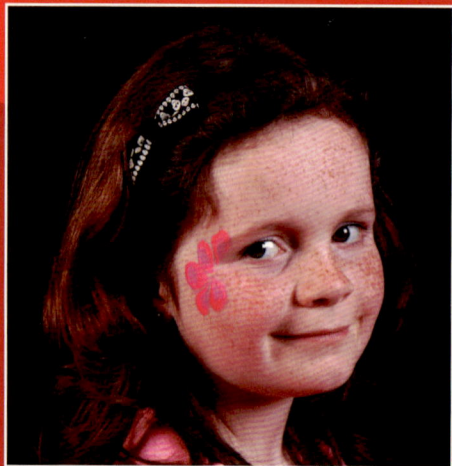

1 With a filbert brush double loaded with light and dark pink, make five petals in a fan shape on one side of the face by pressing the brush down on the skin.

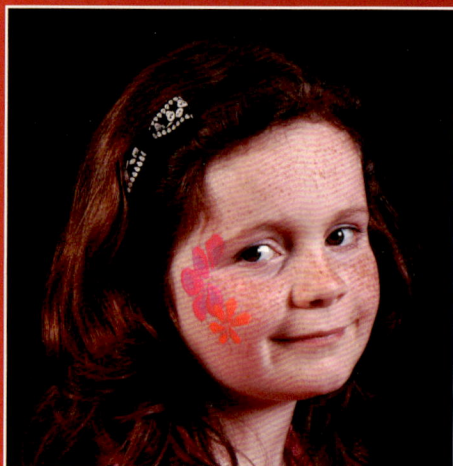

2 Using the same technique, paint another flower directly underneath the pink one in bright orange.

3 Add foliage by using a large round brush loaded with green paint. Add a touch of yellow to the green to add interest. With a fine round brush, add red dots to the centre of the flowers.

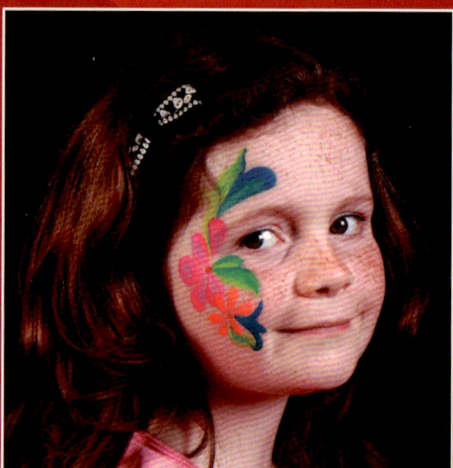

4 Using a large round brush loaded with dark teal, add more foliage in various shapes.

Rainbow Cat

Model: Naomi

Kryolan colours: yellow 509, red 080, pink R30,
blue BL10, green 511, orange 288, black 071, white 070

1 Choose a variety of colours from the rainbow to make a bright and colourful base. Sponge the colours from the centre of the face in a mask shape, leaving the edges and lower half of the face unpainted.

2 With a medium round brush loaded with black, paint thin to thick to thin strokes to create tiger stripes above the eyes. Paint in a small black nose, outline the muzzle and add small black dots for the whiskers.

3 Continuing with the medium round brush, paint tiger stripes on the forehead in a vertical pattern. Paint three eyelashes at the corner of each eye.

4 Paint tiger stripes on the cheeks and open horseshoe shapes around the eyes to create cheetah spots. Add irregular strokes around the edge of the design to indicate fur.

Witch's Web

Model: Emma

Kryolan colours: white 070, green Interferenz GB, black 071

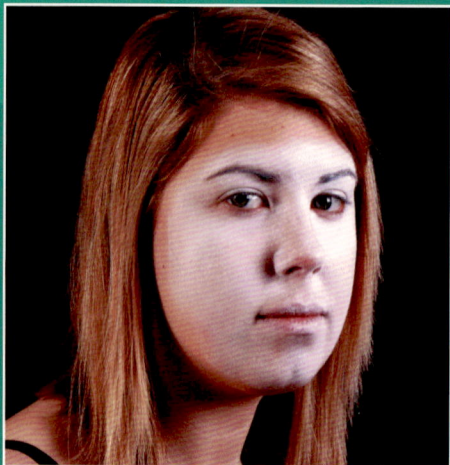

1 Load a sponge with white and cover the whole face, taking care to create a smooth base. Don't forget to pay attention to underneath the eyes and the creases either side of the nose.

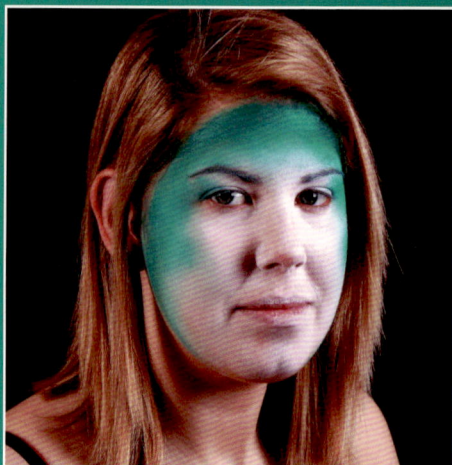

2 Outline the forehead and cheeks in metallic green. Drag the green into the white and then with the sponge loaded with white, drag the white into the green for a seamless finish.

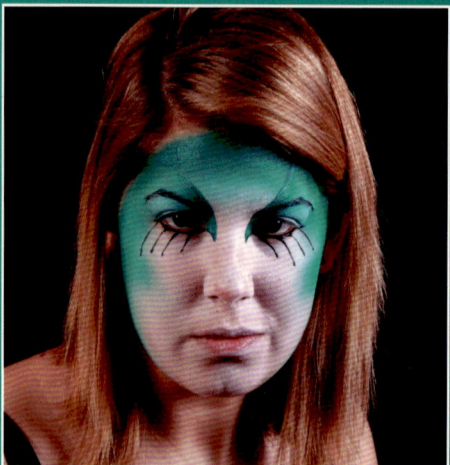

3 Using a round brush loaded with green, paint arches over the eyes from the bridge of the nose. Paint the eyebrows black, adding an exaggerated arch to the natural eyebrow line. To underline the eyelids, ask the model to look up and sweep the paint across in an even brush stroke. Add lines of different lengths underneath the eyes ending in small dots.

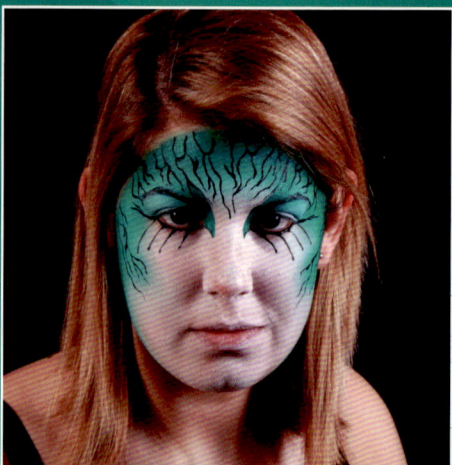

4 Have fun when creating the web patterns. Start from the forehead and twist the brush around to achieve different line thicknesses. Repeat the same method on the cheek area.

5 Paint the lips green and outline in black. With a clean fine brush, drag the black into the green to shade. Add some wispy webs coming out from the corners of the mouth. Finish the webs with a sparkly liquid glitter. Spooky!

Mischevious Monster
Model: Oscar

Kryolan colours: yellow 509, green GR42, red 080, brown 041, black 071, white 070

1 Double load a sponge with yellow and green. Apply the paint to the middle of the face and cheeks, and above the eyebrows.

2 With a large round brush loaded with white, paint teardrop shapes around the edge of the design for horns and teeth.

3 Outline the horns and teeth in black using a fine brush. Outline the main part of the design with fine short brush strokes to create a jagged edge. Finish each stroke with a line going towards the centre of the face.

4 Paint curved shapes in black down the bridge of the nose to create a monster nose and add irregular-shaped spots on the cheeks and forehead. With a dry brush, add a little brown to the base of the teeth and horns and paint the bottom lip in brown. Add some black lines around the muzzle area.

Princess Mermaid

Model: Maddie

Kryolan colours: Interferenz Silber, pink R30, blue G82, blue 510

1 Sponge a perfect circle of shimmer white on the whole face. Apply a little pink around the edge of the circle and blend together.

2 Use a round brush to paint darker pink on the eyelids. Paint the lips with the same shade of pink.

3 With a large brush paint a scallop-shaped line across the middle of the forehead in bright blue. With a sponge, blend the blue into the pink.

4 Load a brush with dark blue and create teardrops on the forehead and at the corners of the eyes. Add decorative twists and curls down the cheeks in a line.

Scary Skull

Model: Oscar

Kryolan colours: brown 503, black 071, white 070

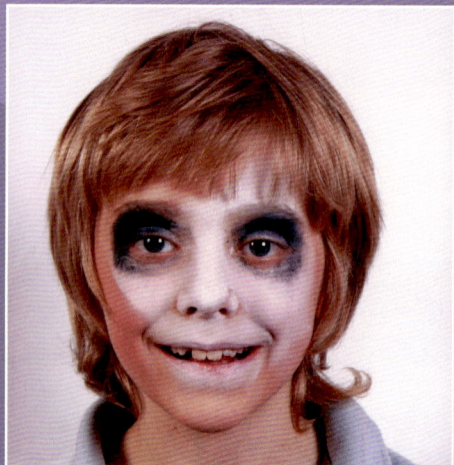

1 Using a sponge loaded with white, sponge an irregular shape across most of the face. Load a dry sponge with black and add patchy black shadows over the eye area for a sunken appearance.

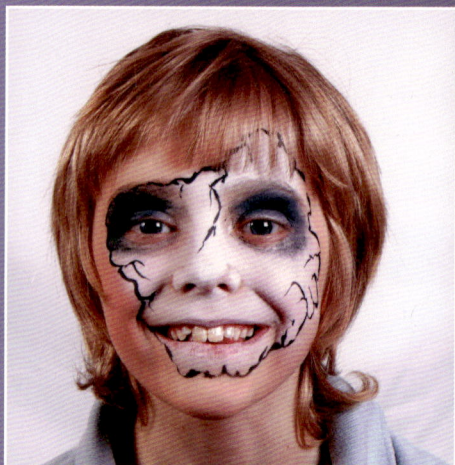

2 With a fine brush loaded with black, outline the white base with a jagged pattern to create a cracked bone look. Extend some of the lines into the face.

3 Add two black triangles for the nose. Using a filbert brush, mix up some thick white paint and paint teeth on top of the lips.

4 Outline the teeth in black, making points on the top edge of each tooth.

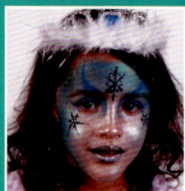

Snowflake Fairy

Model: Mia

Kryolan colours: Interferenz Silber,
blue Interferenz GB, blue 510, Metallic Silber, black 071

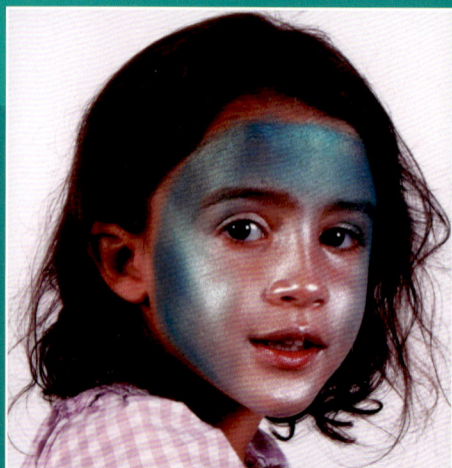

1 Sponge a base of sparkle white all over the face. Add light blue across the forehead, around the eyes and the edges of the face sweeping towards the jaw line.

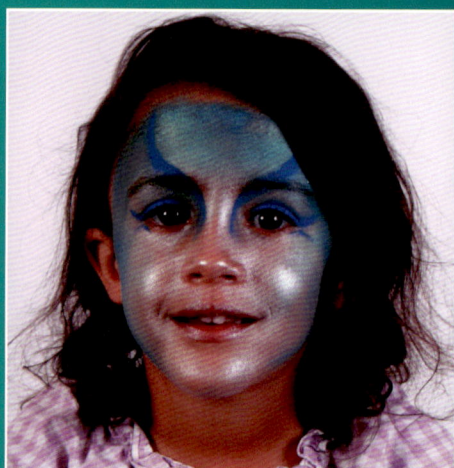

2 With a brush apply dark blue over the eyelids, finishing with an upwards flick. Apply dark blue from the bridge of the nose towards the eyebrows and up the forehead. Blend with a dry sponge.

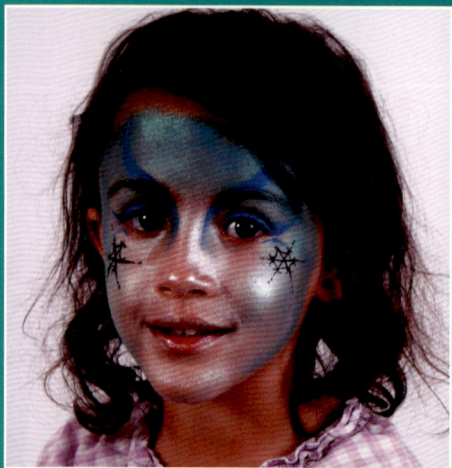

3 Using a fine round brush, add decorative snowflakes on each cheek. Remember snowflakes can be any shape!

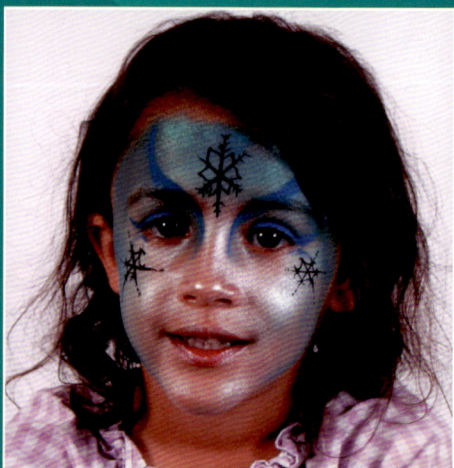

4 Add another snowflake to the centre of the forehead.

Tropical Twist
Model: Holly

Kryolan colours: Interferenz Perlmutt, pink R30, green 095, orange 288, red 080, yellow 509, blue BL10, black 071, white 070

1 Sponge a sparkly iridescent paint onto one cheek and the forehead. Paint an orange circle above the eyebrow for the sun. Sponge red, yellow and blue onto the cheek to create a sunset.

2 With a medium round brush loaded with light and dark pink, make the shape of two flowers on the temple area. Add green leaves to the flowers.

3 Outline the flowers and leaves in black and add some white highlights. Paint red on the top edge of the sun and blend in to the orange for depth.

4 Load a very fine brush with black and paint in an island and palm trees on the cheek, then add some birds flying over the sun. Keep your brush strokes clean and crisp.

Cheeky Cheetah

Model: Josh

Kryolan colours: brown 041, yellow 509,
black 071, white 070, Interferenz Bronze

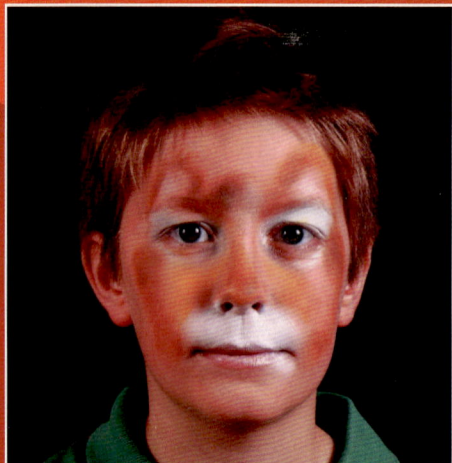

1 Load a sponge with white and apply above the mouth to create a muzzle. Add white to the eyelids sweeping up and outwards. With a sponge loaded with brown, paint the basic shape of the cheetah. Add yellow to the centre of the face and blend into the brown.

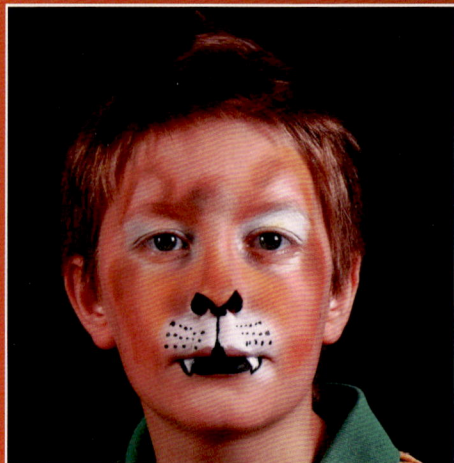

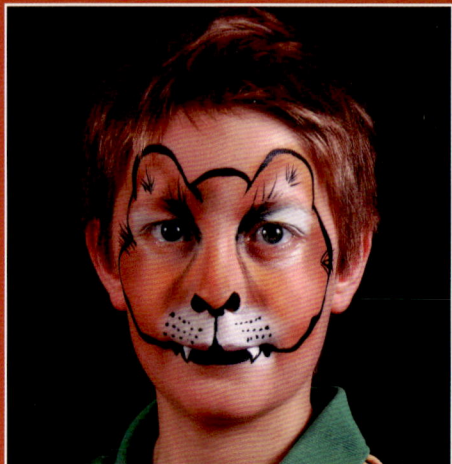

2 Load a sponge with white and apply above the mouth to create a muzzle. Add white to the eyelids sweeping up and outwards. With a sponge loaded with brown, paint the basic shape of the cheetah. Add yellow to the centre of the face and blend into the brown.

3 Outline the design in black. To create fur, paint wispy brush strokes to the side of the cheeks, forehead and eyebrows. Lightly shade down the nose and cheeks.

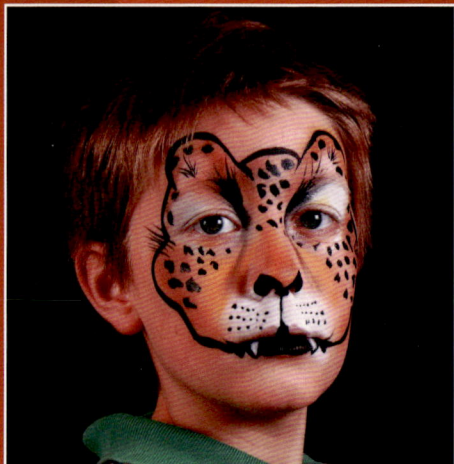

4 Paint irregular spots on the forehead, cheeks and ears for cheetah markings.

5 Embellish the cheetah markings with bronze or gold dots and highlight the bottom lip. Who said the lion is the king of the jungle?

Dreamy Dolphins

Model: Jasmine

Kryolan Colours: Interferenz Silber, Interferenz GB, blue G82, blue 510, Metallic Silber, white 070

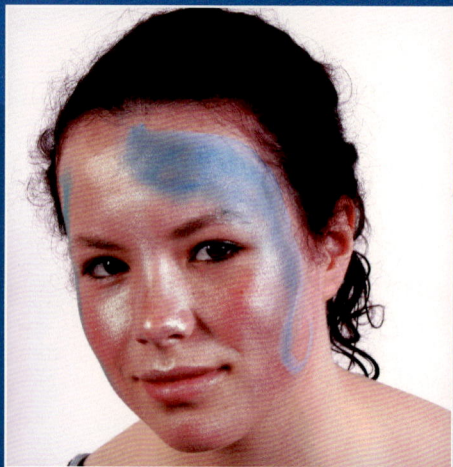

1 Sponge an iridescent sparkly paint all over the face. Load a sponge with light blue and sweep colour down the edge of each side of the face. Start with a wide band on the forehead and finish with a curl shape on the bottom of the cheek.

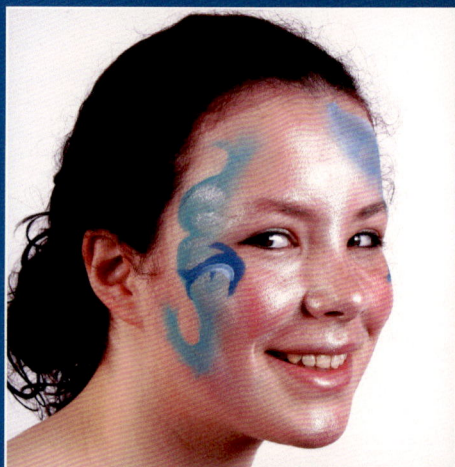

2 With a medium round brush loaded with dark blue, paint a comma shape on each cheek, adding a nose, fins and tail to make a dolphin shape. Add a white highlight to each dolphin's belly.

3 Using a medium round brush, add some curls and swirls above and below the dolphins. Add small groups of turquoise bubbles.

4 With a fine brush loaded with white, add more curls and swirls over the top of the blue ones, in an irregular pattern. Add highlights to the bubbles and small clusters of white dots around the design. Paint a small black dot for the dolphin's eye.

Punky Princess

Model: Louise

Kryolan colours: green 511, green GR42, pink R30, blue BL10, burgundy Altrot, yellow 509, orange 288, black 071, white 070

1 With a large round brush loaded with light green, paint an irregular star shape over one eye. Outline with a dark green and add dots radiating from the points.

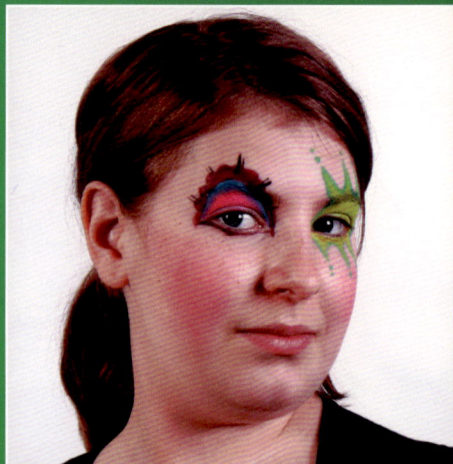

2 On the other eye, sponge bright pink over the eyelid. With a brush, paint a semi-circle in bright blue. Add a scalloped outline in dark purple and line underneath the eye. With a fine brush, paint random dash marks on the scalloped edge.

3 Add a patch on one cheek by painting a square in yellow. Outline in bright orange. Add dashes and dots in black using a fine brush.

4 For the other cheek, paint a bright pink heart with a brush. Outline in bright purple. Add white dots and dashes.

Carnival Mask

Model: Jasmine

Kryolan colours: green 511, blue BL10,
white 070, black 071, blue Interferenz BG

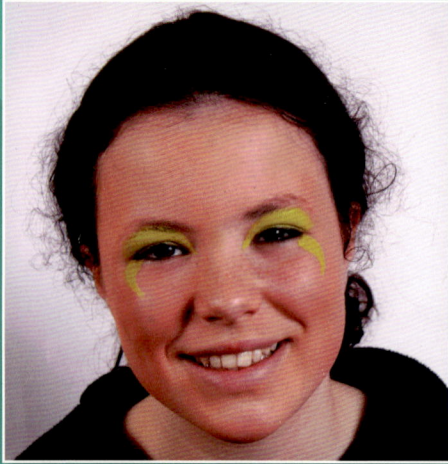

1 To make this design 'pop', sponge on a foundation base of natural-coloured face paint before painting the mask. With a large round brush, paint green on the eyelids and add a curved teardrop shape under each eye.

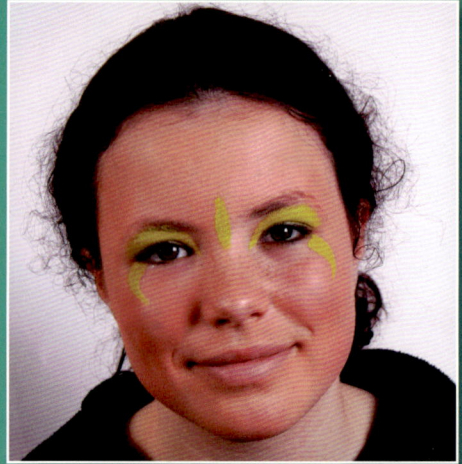

2 In the same colour, add a large teardrop in the centre of the forehead.

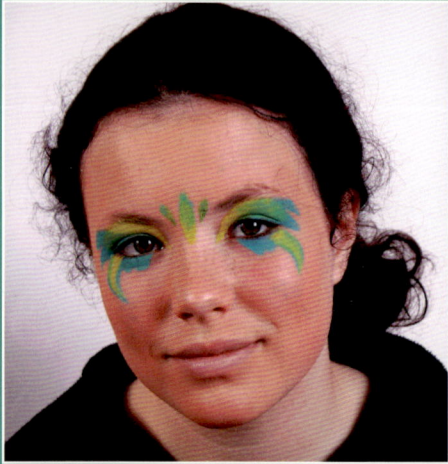

3 With a bright teal blue, paint the shape of the mask and blend into the green.

4 Outline the whole design with bold white brush strokes. Try to ensure that the brush strokes end in curved points. Add two white swirls on the forehead.

With the emphasis on fun, *Fast Fun Faces* gives you a diverse range of ideas to please girls and boys of all ages. The experienced team behind *Illusion*, Claire Pick and Julie Oliver, have created 29 exciting designs based on their knowledge of the faces children like the most. And understanding the importance of speed, each design can be completed very quickly.

With easy-to-follow staged pictures, clear photography and simple instructions this book offers something for everyone – from the novice to the expert face painter. Its practical style makes it the ideal companion on a professional job but also invaluable for anyone wanting to paint for the first time.

Following on from the success of *Illusion and Friends* this is the latest book from the *Illusion* team.

KRYOLAN
PROFESSIONAL MAKE-UP

ISBN 978-0-9555585-2-8

9 780955 558528